F

Stabilizers

Carry-Along Reference Guide

by Sue O'Very-Pruitt

POCKET GUIDE TO STABILIZERS

Landauer Publishing, www.landauerpub.com, is an imprint of Fox Chapel Publishing Company, Inc.

Copyright © 2020 by Sue O'Very-Pruitt and Fox Chapel Publishing Company, Inc., 903 Square Street, Mount Joy, PA 17552.

Project Team
Editorial Director: Kerry Bogert
Editor: Amy Deputato
Copy Editor: Hayley DeBerard
Designer: Mary Ann Kahn
Photographs by Sue O'Very-Pruitt and Heidi O'Very

ISBN 978-1-947163-44-7

Library of Congress Cataloging-in-Publication Data

Names: O'Very-Pruitt, Sue, author.
Title: Pocket guide to stabilizers / by Sue O'Very-Pruitt.
Description: Mount Joy, PA : Fox Chapel Publishing, 2020. | Includes index.
 | Summary: "The author presents an illustrated guide to the different
 types of stabilizers for embroidery projects, including how to use them,
 the types of projects for which they work best, and how to handle and
 store them"-- Provided by publisher.
Identifiers: LCCN 2020027256 (print) | LCCN 2020027257 (ebook) | ISBN
 9781947163447 | ISBN 9781607658177 (ebook)
Subjects: LCSH: Embroidery--Equipment and supplies.
Classification: LCC TT777 .094 2020 (print) | LCC TT777 (ebook) | DDC
 746.44--dc23
LC record available at https://lccn.loc.gov/2020027256
LC ebook record available at https://lccn.loc.gov/2020027257

We are always looking for talented authors. To submit an idea,
please send a brief inquiry to acquisitions@foxchapelpublishing.com.

Printed in China
23 22 21 20   2 4 6 8 10 9 7 5 3 1

Contents

Introduction

What is a stabilizer? A stabilizer is a foundation used in machine embroidery that supports the material during the embroidery stitching process. Stabilizers keep your materials from stretching, puckering, or becoming too stiff. Some stabilizers remain under the stitches of finished projects while others are washed away, cut out, torn away, or even ironed away. Choosing the best stabilizer for the type of material can make or break the finished appearance of the project. To achieve professional results, you must choose not only a suitable embroidery design but also the most appropriate stabilizer. Not every design is intended to be embroidered on every type of material, so a good rule of thumb is the thinner the material, the less dense the design should be per square inch.

In this pocket guide, I will:

- discuss the basic types of stabilizers, the different kinds within each category, and a limited list of stabilizer brands/ product names for each type
- show the uses for each type of stabilizer
- offer tips for working with each type of stabilizer
- break down a list of material types and suggested stabilizers for each
- recommend hooping methods for the materials and stabilizers
- cover the basics of thread, needles, and ways to adhere materials to stabilizers
- present a stabilizer cheat sheet

Choose your stabilizer based on the requirements of your project and the materials.

Using This Guide

This pocket guide may be little, but it is packed full of tips and tricks to help you use embroidery stabilizers successfully. At the end of the description of each type of stabilizer, there will be additional tips, best hooping practices, and more. The one tip I include here is to start yourself a stabilizer notebook. Keep track of the stabilizers, designs, needles, and thread used. Pay attention to the brands you really like and where you purchased them. All these notes will come in handy when you least expect it, and you will thank me for it.

   This pocket guide is designed to show the basics of which stabilizers to use with which materials in a quick reference manner. The idea is to help you consider your options while shopping for stabilizers, show you how to hoop materials, and instruct you in removing stabilizers after your embroidery is complete. Each section of Guide to Stabilizer Types and Uses (beginning on page 32) is dedicated to a certain type of stabilizer, breaking down the different varieties of that stabilizer and listing a limited number of brands. Many brands offer detailed instructions and excellent education on their websites, so it is a good idea to research their recommendations when using their brands.

   Please know that there are numerous possibilities for techniques, stabilizers, materials, and designs. Use this pocket guide as a reference, because not all stabilizers (even if they look alike) are created equal. Testing the stabilizer, material, and design is always the best way to decide on the final combination.

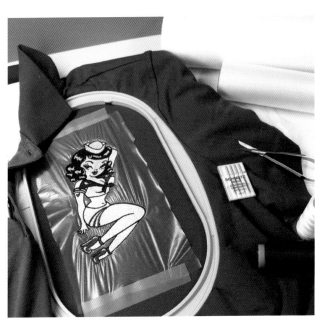

Professional-looking embroidery starts with a good design and the right supplies. Design from Suzy Sailor by Fluff, OESD.

Before You Begin

When you are first learning machine embroidery, the variety of stabilizers may seem overwhelming. You might be wondering, *Why are there so many stabilizers, and how do I choose?*

There are so many types of stabilizers because there are so many types of materials and embroidery designs, as well as various ways to "hoop" materials. Some areas of fabric, such as napkin corners and shirt collars, cannot be hooped.

It is a good idea to have a stash of test materials to try out before stitching on your real project. The next time you are at the discount store, grab some napkins, towels, and T-shirts to use for test stitching. Most importantly, enjoy trying new materials, embrace the mistakes, and have fun!

BACKINGS VERSUS TOPPINGS

Before we discuss the various types of stabilizers, it is important to understand where they are applied. There are two options: either on the back of the material (backings) or on top of the material (toppings). Backings are more common, as nearly every embroidery project requires some sort of stabilization. Toppings are usually used in conjunction with backings. Most every type of stabilizer can be used as a backing, while only a few are appropriate as toppings.

This pocket guide discusses backings and toppings when referring to different types of stabilizers and their application. For example, when embroidering a terrycloth towel, the backing is a tear-away and the topping is a wash-away.

Stabilizer is most commonly used on the back of materials, but some projects call for toppings as well.

Basic Types of Stabilizers

When your embroidery project is complete, ideally the stabilizer will be either hidden or completely removed. Even though there are dozens of brands and hundreds of different stabilizers on the market, there really are only five different categories, or types.

Tear-away: Even though tear-away is not paper, at first glance it appears to have a paper-like texture. Tear-away ranges from light to heavy and can be layered to help stabilize many materials. Tear-away is removed from around the design once stitching is complete, and the rest will remain under the stitches for the life of the project.

Cut-away: This type of stabilizer is often confused with interfacing because it has a similar look and feel. Cut-away is a non-woven, smooth mixture of polyester fibers and other binders. Once stitching is complete, cut this stabilizer away around the stitches. The rest of the stabilizer will remain under the stitches for the life of the project.

Wash-away: There are a couple of kinds of wash-away stabilizers. Some are clear and others are mesh style. Some tear away first and then are washed away; others need to be cut away and then washed. No matter which wash-away you use, you will end up washing the stabilizer out of the finished project. Follow the manufacturer's removal instructions. Most of the time, massaging the stitches under warm running water will loosen the wash-away, and eventually it will completely dissolve.

Heat-away: All varieties of heat-away stabilizer are clear and can be torn away, with the leftover pieces removed with the heat of an iron. Follow the manufacturer's removal instructions.

Specialty: The stabilizers that fit into this category provide some type of unique functionality that none of the previously mentioned types do. Some are used in addition to the other types of stabilizers, and some stand alone. I will discuss the most popular specialty types on the market and uses for each.

Within each type of stabilizer, there are many kinds. Two of the more commonly used kinds are fusible and sticky.

Fusible: Fuse (with an iron) this stabilizer to the wrong side of the material, which temporarily alters the body of the material to help prevent shifting. For added stabilization, you can place a piece of stabilizer under the hoop (floating) or iron on two layers of the fusible stabilizer.

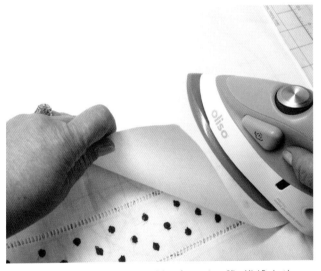

Fusible stabilizer is attached temporarily with heat from an iron. Oliso Mini Project Iron; towel from All About Blanks.

Sticky: This is an adhesive stabilizer with a paper backing; hoop it with the paper side facing up. Use a straight pin to score the paper without tearing into the adhesive layer and then remove the paper, exposing the adhesive. You then place the material on the sticky side of the stabilizer and embroider it. Once you've finished stitching, remove the material/stabilizer from the hoop and then remove the stabilizer from the material based on what type of stabilizer it is: tear-away, wash-away, or cut-away. In some cases, additional stabilization might be required, such as a fusible tear-away or cut-away.

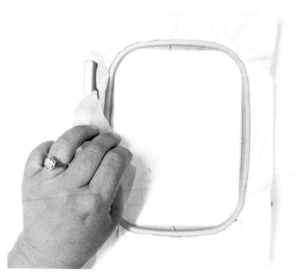

Sticky stabilizer helps when hooping difficult items in place for embroidery.

HOOPING VERSUS FLOATING

To stitch the design onto the material, something must be inside the embroidery hoop, and it must be attached in some manner. Most stabilizer manufacturers recommend that you have at least 1 to 2 inches (2.5 to 5cm) of stabilizer surrounding the outside of the hoop while you are embroidering.

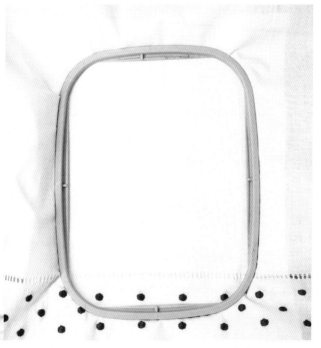

An example of hooping: the material and stabilizer together inside the hoop.

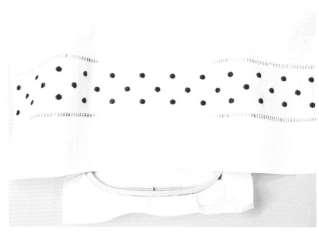

An example of floating: hooped stabilizer with the material placed on top.

Either sandwich the stabilizer and material together inside the hoop (hooping) or hoop the stabilizer with the material floating on top of the stabilizer (floating).

Not every material or stabilizer or project is suited for both methods. For example, a bath towel is very thick and difficult to hoop; plus, the hoop would leave hoop marks (sometimes referred to as hoop burn) on the material. In this case, you would hoop the stabilizer and float the towel on top. There are many methods of attaching the towel to the stabilizer so that it does not shift while being embroidered. See the Adhesives section (page 23) for suggested ways to adhere materials to stabilizers.

You can place another piece of stabilizer under the hoop, loose and floating, either with material and stabilizer hooped together or when only the stabilizer is hooped and the material is floating on top. This step adds extra stabilization without the stabilizer being inside the hoop.

In this example, the material floats on top of the hoop, one piece of stabilizer is hooped, and an additional piece floats under the hoop for added stabilization. Design from Teen Rock by OESD.

When cutting your material, take into account that you should leave 1 to 2 inches (2.5 to 5cm) of fabric outside the hoop.

Basic Types of Materials

From linen to faux fur, every material must somehow be stabilized when adding machine embroidery to it. Here are the five most common types of materials:

Woven: Most woven materials have little to no stretch:

- Quilting cotton
- Denim
- Canvas
- Linen
- Gauze

Denim is a popular woven fabric for embroidered clothing and accessories.

Knit: Most knit materials have 20 percent or higher stretch:
- Baby onesie/light T-shirt
- Pique polo/heavy T-shirt/sweatshirt
- Swimwear
- Performance wear

Napped: Any material with a loft or pile:
- Terrycloth (e.g., bath towel)
- Faux fur/velvet
- Fleece/minky

Sheer: Any material that is fully or partially see-through:
- Organza/chiffon
- Lace/netting

Materials such as Luxe Cuddle® can at first glance be intimidating to embroider on, but once you know the tricks, it's pretty easy and rewarding.

Embroidery adds a special touch to all types of fabrics. Designs (clockwise from bottom left) from: Crib Hair Don't Care (bib) by Sue O'Very Designs; Suzy Sailor (polo shirt) by Fluff, OESD; Mermaid at Heart (swimsuit) by Scissortail Stitches; All a Twitter by Kari Carr, OESD (linen towel from All About Blanks); Enchanted Baby (onesie) by Sue O'Very Designs; Teen Rock (pillow) by OESD on Luxe Cuddle® fabric in Rose Fuchsia from Shannon Fabrics.

Non-woven: Any material with little to no woven structure. Even though some non-woven materials might have a woven backing, the raw edges will not fray when you cut around the material. These are heavier materials that are usually difficult to hoop:

- Cork
- Vinyl
- Pet screen

In some cases, the project or technique being used, rather than the material, will determine the type of stabilizer needed. The following are a few such cases:

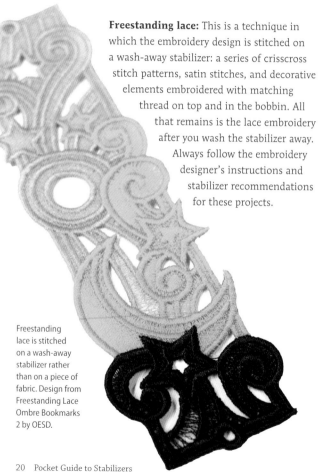

Freestanding lace: This is a technique in which the embroidery design is stitched on a wash-away stabilizer: a series of crisscross stitch patterns, satin stitches, and decorative elements embroidered with matching thread on top and in the bobbin. All that remains is the lace embroidery after you wash the stabilizer away. Always follow the embroidery designer's instructions and stabilizer recommendations for these projects.

Freestanding lace is stitched on a wash-away stabilizer rather than on a piece of fabric. Design from Freestanding Lace Ombre Bookmarks 2 by OESD.

Hard-to-hoop items: This refers to anything that is difficult to put into the hoop without taking the project apart, e.g., napkin corners, socks, cuffs, collars, blank luggage tags, and other blank ready-made items. These all require some sort of sticky stabilizer, but the type of stabilizer (tear-away, cut-away, wash-away, or heat-away) will depend on the type of material.

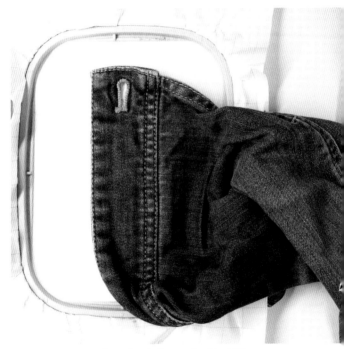

Hard-to-hoop projects, such as cuffs and collars, require sticky stabilizer.

In-the-Hoop projects: These are typically projects that are completely or nearly completely constructed inside the embroidery hoop, e.g., zipper purses, coin purses, mug rugs, key fobs, and about a million other things. There are many different designs and many different techniques for constructing them. An In-the-Hoop project is subject to not only the type of fabric but also the final construction method. My best suggestion is to follow the designer's instructions exactly when trying a project for the first time; if you want to make alterations, do so the next time making the project.

Use In-the-Hoop embroidery for a range of projects. Designs clockwise from left: Hexi Coin Purse, Sassy Stripe (pouch), and Monogram Mug Mat all by Sue O'Very Designs.

ADHESIVES

When floating material on top of the stabilizer or under the hoop, you need a way of keeping everything in place to prevent shifting and potentially jamming the machine. The following are just a few of the basics:

Auto-basting: Many machines offer a built-in basting stitch that surrounds the outside of the embroidery area. If your machine does not offer a built-in stitch, you can find aftermarket machine-embroidery software that will add it to your embroidery designs. Check your machine's user manual or ask your local shop about auto-basting.

Auto-basting stitches the stabilizer around the outside of the embroidery area.

Embroidery spray adhesive: A light coat of adhesive spray should be sprayed directly onto the stabilizer, not onto the material, as the spray might leave spots. Always spray away from your embroidery machine so the sticky residue does not settle on your machine or get into the internal parts. Also try to avoid spraying directly onto the hoop; if the hoop becomes sticky, use an adhesive remover such as GooGone®. Be sure to always spray in a well-ventilated area. Products include:

- Odif—505® Temporary Adhesive
- Sulky®—KK 2000™
- Dritz®—Spray Adhesive

Fabric glue pen/stick: Use wash-away glue pens/sticks designed for fabric. Avoid paper glue pens/sticks because they can cause the needle and your bobbin area to get gummed up. Keep the lid on the fabric glue when not in use to keep it from drying out. Products include:

- Sewline™—Water Soluble Glue Pen: This pen is refillable and has a smaller circumference than a stick, which can work well in tiny areas of machine embroidery.
- Dritz®—Fabric Glue Stick: This non-refillable stick has a larger circumference, which is ideal for when you have larger areas to cover in hoops.

Clips: When spray or glue is not an option, clips can be a good solution. Make sure the presser foot and needle have clearance on the clips so as not to hurt the machine or break a needle. Products include:

- Clover—Wonder Clips®: These plastic clips have a wide opening. The bottom side lays flat, whereas the top has an angle, making it easy to pick up the clips. Use them vertically on the sides of the hoop to hold the material to the hoop or, better yet, clip them to the stabilizer.

- SewTites®: These two-piece magnetic clips hold the stabilizer and material together without leaving residue or pin holes. The top is a piece of plastic with magnets on one side. The bottom is a flat metal piece that holds the layers together. SewTites® come in a variety of sizes to hold materials of different weights and configurations together in the embroidery hoop.

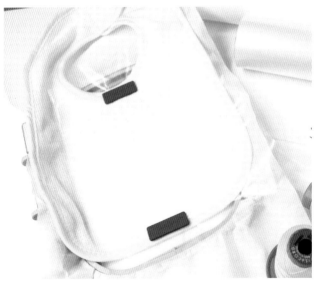

SewTites are placed on the top and bottom of the layers, holding everything together magnetically.

Tape: Sometimes all you need is a piece of tape to hold your material in place. There are different kinds of tape, including:

- Wash-away: As indicated by its name, this tape will disappear after washing, preventing it from getting trapped under the stitches permanently. It is ideal for projects where a wash-away stabilizer is used, and it can be used on the front and back of the hoop. When used on the back of the hoop, this tape often shifts when the machine is stitching, but extending the tape onto the plastic of the hoop can help prevent this.

- Clear adhesive: Use a matte-finished invisible tape instead of transparent tape. If the tape does get caught in the stitches, it easily perforates and can be removed. Test the tape-and-material combination to make sure no sticky residue is left on the materials. If the tape leaves a residue, simply remove some of the residue by placing the tape onto a piece of fleece a few times to "un-stick" the tape. This is a good option for holding material to stabilizers on the front and back of the hoop. Extend the tape onto the plastic of the hoop and secure.

- Painter's tape: This is a low-adhesive tape used for painting and found in the hardware store; it works great when adhering materials to stabilizers on the front of the hoop. On the back of the hoop, this tape often shifts when the machine is stitching.

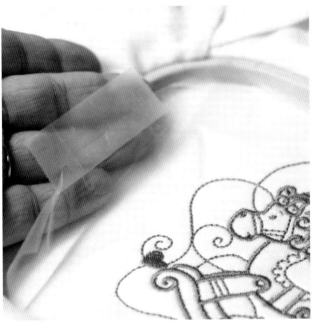

Low-adhesive tape is an option for holding layers together. Design from Enchanted Baby by Sue O'Very Designs.

NEEDLES AND THREAD

There are special needles and thread designed to work with machine embroidery. I use three types of needles and four types of thread when machine embroidering. There are many options, so I recommend asking your local shop to show you their favorites and experimenting to discover yours.

Needles

There are many brands of sewing-machine needles on the market, and I've found that SCHMETZ® needles work with all brands consistently. There are also many types of needles, but as this is a basic guide to machine embroidery, I've listed the three most common types here. Ask your local shop which needles they suggest for your brand of machine.

Embroidery 75/11: The most common needle for machine embroidery, this works well on most light- to medium-weight materials. The eye of the needle is short and wide, allowing specialty threads to glide through at high speeds. This needle is great for woven, knit, napped, and sheer materials. Consider using an Embroidery 90/14 for heavier-weight materials.

Topstitch 80/12: This needle is designed to work well with heavy threads to achieve perfect stitches. The eye of the needle is extra-long and wide, allowing thread to glide through easily at the high speed of machine embroidery. This needle is excellent with all materials and is my personal "go-to" needle. It is the best solution when working with non-woven materials such as cork and vinyl.

Metallic 80/12: Ideal for metallic and other specialty threads, this needle has a long eye that helps prevent shredding and breaking of sensitive metallic threads. It works with most materials, but consider using a Metallic 90/14 for heavier-weight materials.

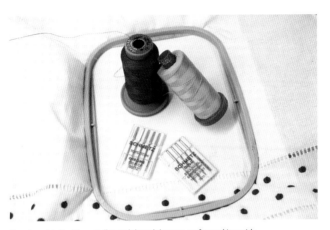

Experiment to find the needles and thread that you prefer working with.

Thread

When embroidering, your top thread will be either 40 or 50 weight, and the bobbin will usually be 60 weight. Ask your local shop which type of top and bobbin thread are best for your machine. There are many brands, weights, and fiber contents on the market. Once you find which brand works best for you, have fun and start collecting! Threads are like paints for a canvas, and it's important to remember that the machine is colorblind, so even if the machine shows an embroidery thread color, it is only a suggestion. You are the designer and can use whichever color you prefer. Here are the five most popular types of thread.

60-weight bobbin thread: This thinner weight is for the bobbin only. It comes on a spool from which you wind your own bobbin, or some brands will accept pre-wound bobbins. Ask your local shop what works best on your embroidery machine.

40-weight polyester: Strong and colorfast, this thread will not bleed onto materials, has medium shine, and is durable in washing and drying.

40-weight rayon: Weaker and not colorfast, this thread can potentially bleed onto materials, has high shine, and is semi-durable in washing and drying.

50-weight cotton: Strong and colorfast, this thread will not bleed onto materials and has no shine—instead, it offers a matte finish. It is durable in washing and drying.

Metallic, various weights and textures: There is much variety in metallic threads: wiry, smoother, scratchy, glittery, and more. Always use the metallic needle when stitching with a metallic thread. Most metallics are colorfast and will not bleed onto materials; they have a high shine and are semi-durable in washing and drying.

STORAGE

How you decide to store your stabilizer has a lot to do with how much room you have, the packaging of the stabilizers, and where you live in the world. Yes, your climate can influence how stabilizers react. For example, in very humid climates, it is a good idea to keep water-soluble stabilizers in an airtight container.

Stabilizers are sold a few different ways: in rolls, packages, and plastic tubes, and by the yard. Take your stabilizers' original packaging into consideration when deciding how to best store them.

Even in a small sewing room, you can keep your stabilizers orderly and tidy. When storing rolls and plastic tubes, you can use a hanging shoe organizer or wine rack, or even place them nicely in deep drawers or tubs. Most brands include instructions on the backside of the packaging/cover. Either keep the packaging on the outside of the roll and wrap with low-adhesive tape (like painter's tape) or use a piece of clear vinyl to wrap the roll and then wrap the vinyl on to itself. You can also roll the instructions and tuck them inside the cardboard tube. You might notice that some brands of stabilizers color-code their packaging, e.g., blue for wash-away. This can be extremely helpful when searching through packaging to find the type of stabilizer you need.

When storing stabilizer that comes in packages or by the yard, neatly fold the stabilizer to fit into a large zip-top plastic bag. Remember to always keep the packaging and instructions.

HOW IT'S SOLD

Rolls versus yardage? You might be wondering if there is an advantage to buying one over the other. It really comes down to the size of the hoop you are using. Remember, I mentioned that most manufacturers recommend having 1 to 2 inches (2.5 to 5cm) of stabilizer on the outside of your hoop. Therefore, I recommend that you purchase stabilizer based on your most frequently used hoops. I personally prefer the rolls that are 9 to 12 inches (23 to 30mm) wide, as this covers the hoops that I use the most.

Guide to Stabilizer Types and Uses

There are dozens of brands and hundreds of stabilizers on the market, and they can all be narrowed down into these five types:

- ▶ TEAR-AWAY
- ▶ CUT-AWAY
- ▶ WASH-AWAY
- ▶ HEAT-AWAY
- ▶ SPECIALTY

All a Twitter by Kari Carr, OESD.

TEAR-AWAY

About

Tear-away stabilizers are ideal for woven materials with little to no stretch. They come in a variety of kinds, which you will choose depending on how your material/project needs to be hooped, and in various weights, which you will choose based on how dense the design is. After you finish stitching, remove the tear-away from around the outside of the embroidery design. The stabilizer that is under the stitches will remain there for the life of the project. When using more than one layer of tear-away, remove one layer at a time, always supporting the stitches as you tear. Some brands of stabilizer are non-directional, meaning that you can tear them away from every direction, whereas you may find that other brands are more difficult to tear away from some angles.

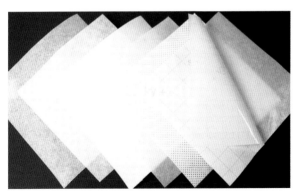

As the name suggests, remove tear-away stabilizer by tearing around the outside of the embroidery design.

Varieties

Lightweight: Ideal for lightweight woven materials with low stitch-count designs, such as linen, gauze, and even vinyl. This stabilizer is often hooped with the material, or a single layer can be floated under the hoop when it is used in combination with another stabilizer.

- OESD™—Light Weight
- Exquisite® by dime—Light Tearaway
- Sulky®—Tear-Easy™

Medium weight: Ideal for medium-weight materials with medium- to higher-density designs. Great with quilting cotton, denim, canvas, linen, terrycloth, fleece, minky, cork, and vinyl. This stabilizer is often hooped with the material, or a single layer can be floated under the hoop when it is used in combination with another stabilizer.

- OESD™
  - Medium Weight, Black (use on dark woven materials)
  - Ultra Clean and Tear
- Exquisite® by dime
  - Medium Tearaway (Firm)
  - Medium Black Tearaway (Firm)
  - Medium Soft Tearaway
- Sulky®—Stiffy™
- Bosal—Tear Away Medium Weight

Heavy weight: Ideal for higher-density designs with some open areas and for medium- to heavy-weight materials, such as canvas, fleece, and minky. This stabilizer is often hooped with the material, or a single layer can be floated under the hoop when it is used in combination of another stabilizer.

- OESD™—Heavy Weight

- Exquisite® by dime
  - Heavy Tearaway
  - Heavy Soft Tearaway
- Bosal—Tear Away Heavy Weight

Fusible: Iron on and then tear away. Perfect for materials like quilting cotton, linen, and gauze. This stabilizer is designed to be fused to the wrong side of the material and then hooped with the material facing up. When you are done stitching, remove the project from hoop and apply heat with the iron to help remove the fusible stabilizer. Gently hold the stitches and remove the stabilizer by tearing it away. Ideal for medium-density designs; add a second layer for higher-density designs. An added layer of a thinner weight of tear-away can be floated under the hoop.

- OESD™—Ultra Clean and Tear Fusible
- Exquisite® by dime—Fuse 'N Tear
- Sulky®—Totally Stable™

Flame retardant: Perforated medium-weight stabilizer with an incredibly soft hand. Ideal for sleepwear, workwear, and children's wear. Tears easily and cleanly around embroidery. Hoop with the materials; once stitching is complete, gently tear away the stabilizer from the stitches.

- Exquisite® by dime—Safe Tear Flame Retardant
- Bosal—F/R Perforated Tear Away
- The Gypsy Quilter® Stitcher Series Hoop Easy Tear Away

Sticky: Tear-away stabilizer with a paper backing covering the adhesive stabilizer. Hoop the stabilizer with the paper side up, score the paper gently, and remove the paper to expose the adhesive. Place the material on top of the sticky stabilizer and embroider. Once stitching is finished, gently remove the stabilizer by tearing it away from the stitches. Ideal for hard to hoop materials, such as napkin corners or collars. For additional stabilization, float a piece of light- to medium-weight tear-away stabilizer under the hoop. You can also use a fusible tear-away first, and then place the material on the sticky stabilizer. When you are finished stitching, remove each layer of stabilizer individually.

- OESD™:
    - Ultra Clean and Tear Plus (tear-away and wash-away)
    - StabilStick Tear Away
- Exquisite® by dime—Peel 'N Stick
- Sulky®—Sticky + ™
- The Gypsy Quilter® Stitcher Series Hoop Easy Stick & Tear

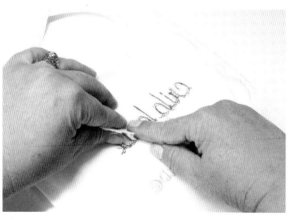

When removing tear-away, hold the stitches with one hand and tear with the other.

TIPS

• When removing the stabilizer, hold the stitches and gently tear away the stabilizer so as not to distort the stitches.

• The more stitches per square inch, the heavier the stabilizer needed. It is often (but not always) better to use more layers of a lighter-weight stabilizer than a single layer of a heavier weight.

• When removing multiple layers of tear-away, remove one layer at a time.

• When removing fusible stabilizer, use the iron to help release the stabilizer.

• Firm versus soft stabilizer:

  ♦ Firm is crisp, it tears apart cleanly, and it sometimes can be stiffer.

  ♦ Soft is flexible and leaves hairy fibers when it tears apart.

• Some brands of tear-away are also somewhat wash-away, so read the packaging.

• Some brands of tear-away become softer with every wash.

• For each brand and type, follow the manufacturer's directions, as they may vary slightly from one to the next.

CUT-AWAY

About

Cut-away stabilizers are ideal for materials with 20 percent or more stretch, such as knits, and can hold a denser design. They come in a variety of kinds to choose from depending on how your material/project needs to be hooped/floated. When you are finished stitching, cut the cut-away around the stitching area, leaving the remaining stabilizer under the stitches for the life of the project. Some brands offer a variety of colors. As a rule, white is ideal for light colors, beige is ideal for white or tan materials, and black is ideal for dark materials.

Use scissors to remove cut-away stabilizer by cutting around the embroidery design.

Varieties

Mesh (sheer): Soft, sheer, strong, and translucent nylon backing to prevent show-through. Each brand's weight of sheer cut-away is slightly different, and some are smoother than others. Ideal for baby onesies, lightweight T-shirts, performance wear, fleece, and minky. Designed to be hooped with the material.

- OESD™:
  - PolyMesh White
  - PolyMesh Beige
  - PolyMesh Black
- Exquisite® by dime:
  - No Show White
  - No Show Beige
  - No Show Black
- Sulky®—Soft 'n Sheer™
- Bosal—No Show Nylon Mesh
- The Gypsy Quilter® Stitcher Series Hoop Easy Sew-In Mesh

Medium weight: Excellent for medium- to heavy-density designs. Ideal for materials including light denim, pique polo, heavy T-shirt, sweatshirt, swimwear, fleece, and minky. Designed to be hooped with the material.

- OESD™—Medium Weight
- Exquisite® by dime—Medium Cutaway
- Sulky®—Cut-Away Plus™
- Bosal—Cut Away Medium Weight

Heavy weight: Use with heavy-density designs. Ideal for denim, pique polo, heavy T-shirt, and sweatshirt materials. Designed to be hooped with the material.

- OESD™:
  - Heavy Weight White

Some brands offer cut-away in a range of colors, including white, beige, and black.

- Heavy Weight Black
- Exquisite® by dime—Heavy Cutaway
- Bosal—Cut Away Heavy Weight

Fusible: Iron-on mesh (sheer). Good for light- to medium-density designs. Ideal for baby onesies, light T-shirts, and even quilting cotton for a soft hand. Apply by fusing to the wrong side of the material and hoop all together. When you are finished stitching, remove the materials the from the hoop, apply heat from the iron to help remove the fusible stabilizer, and cut away.

- OESD™—Fusible PolyMesh

- Exquisite® by dime – Fusible No Show
- Sulky® Soft 'n Sheer Extra™

Sticky: Medium-weight cut-away with an adhesive backing, ideal for knits and stretchy fabrics. Works well for projects that are hard to hoop and made of materials such as light denim, pique polo, heavy T-shirt, and sweatshirt. When finished stitching, remove the stabilizer from the hoop and cut the stabilizer around the stitches.

- OESD™ - StabilStick Cut Away

Small duckbill scissors help you cut close to the stitches. Mini Duck Bill scissors by Famore Cutlery.

TIPS

- To achieve a smooth embroidery surface, spray the stabilizer with a spray adhesive, place it on the wrong side of the material, and then hoop all together.

- When removing cut-away stabilizer, use a pair of small duckbill appliqué scissors. Place the duckbill closest to the material, with the straight edge on the stabilizer, and leave about ⅛" (3.2mm) of stabilizer. If the stabilizer is fusible, use the iron to help release the stabilizer.

- The more stitches per square inch, the heavier the stabilizer needed. It is better to use more layers of a lighter-weight stabilizer than a single layer of a heavier weight.

- When embroidering on a lighter-weight material with a medium- to heavy-density design, a lightweight stabilizer might not be enough. You can add a second layer of cut-away (as shown in the photo), but another option is to use one layer of cut-away and float a piece of lightweight tear-away under the hoop. This will add temporary stabilization while you are stitching the design, but not too much.

- For each brand and type, follow the manufacturer's directions, as they may vary slightly from one to the next.

Use two layers of cut-away, if needed, with lightweight materials.

WASH-AWAY

About

Wash-away stabilizers are used as backings and toppings, depending on the material, project, and application. Ultimately, wash-away is completely removed with water, so test your material to make sure you can wash it. As a backing, wash-away is the preferred stabilizer when both sides of the material are visible, such as with napkins. As a topping, wash-away is fitting because it keeps the stitches from sinking into lofty or napped materials by creating a smooth surface. Wash-away is also used for freestanding lace, as it becomes the foundation that the stitches are built upon, later to be completely removed.

Wash-away is a water-soluble stabilizer that is removed completely by washing the finished project.

Varieties

Light clear: Thin, clear, and smooth. Easily tears away after stitching, and any remaining stabilizer washes out easily. Use it as a topping for materials including denim, linen, gauze, onesie, light T-shirt, pique polo, heavy T-shirt, sweatshirt, swimwear, terrycloth, faux fur, velvet, fleece, minky, lace, netting, cork, and many In-the-Hoop projects. It can also be used as a backing/topping with lighter materials sandwiched in the middle.

- OESD™—StitcH$_2$0 (the presser foot glides easily on top of it)
- Exquisite® by dime—Water Soluble Topping
- Sulky®—Solvy™
- Bosal—Water Soluble
- The Gypsy Quilter® Stitcher Series Hoop Easy Topper

Heavy clear: Heavy, clear, and smooth. Does not tear easily but can be cut around the design area. Cut as close to the stitching as possible, and any remaining stabilizer washes out. Ideal for backings and for freestanding lace.

- OESD™ – BadgeMaster
- Sulky® - Ultra Solvy™

Mesh: Opaque mesh water-soluble stabilizer. Cut around the design area as close to the stitching as possible, and what is not cut away will wash out. Ideal for backings and for freestanding lace. Works well with gauze, organza, chiffon, lace, and netting.

- OESD™— AquaMesh
- Exquisite® by dime— Sew 'N Wash
- Bosal— Wash Away Plus

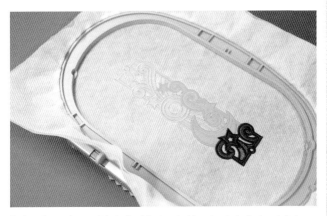
Mesh wash-away is a good choice for delicate materials and projects. Bookmark design from Freestanding Lace Ombre Bookmarks 2 by OESD.

Sticky: Opaque mesh water-soluble stabilizer with adhesive backing; ideal for projects that are hard to hoop. When you are finished stitching, remove the stabilizer from the hoop and cut around the design area as close to the stitching as possible. Any remaining stabilizer will wash out. Ideal for backings and for freestanding lace. Works well with gauze, organza, chiffon, lace, and netting.

- OESD™—AquaMesh Plus
- Exquisite® by dime—Adhesive Sew 'N Wash
- Sulky®—Sticky Fabri-Solvy™
- The Gypsy Quilter® Stitcher Series Hoop Easy Stick & Wash

TIPS

- Most manufacturers recommend storing water-soluble stabilizers in airtight containers. Read the packaging and instructions for storage suggestions.

- When using wash-away as a topping, adhere it to the hoop with a small piece of tape or slightly dampen the corners. This allows the water-soluble stabilizer to stick to the material.

- When using wash-away as a backing, be sure to hoop it nice and taut so it glides on the bed of the machine easily.

- When removing the stabilizer requires scissors, use a pair of small duckbill appliqué scissors. Place the duckbill closest to the material with the straight edge on the stabilizer and leave about ⅛" (3.2mm) of stabilizer. Whatever is not cut away will wash away.

- For each brand and type, follow the manufacturer's directions, as they may vary slightly from one to the next.

HEAT-AWAY

About

Heat-away stabilizers are used as backings and toppings when you don't want to have any traces of leftover stabilizer, and wash-away is not an option.

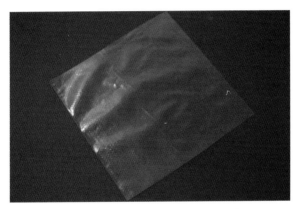

Heat-away is a thin, clear stabilizer that is removed with the heat of an iron.

Varieties

Clear: Thin and clear with a slightly bumpy texture. Tears away after stitching, and any remaining stabilizer is easily removed with the heat of an iron. Use as a topping for materials such as pique polo, heavy T-shirt, sweatshirt, swimwear, terrycloth, faux fur, velvet, fleece, and minky.

- OESD™—Heat2Go
- Exquisite® by dime—Sew 'N Heat
- Sulky®—Heat-Away Clear Film™

TIPS

- Use as a topping for a permanent solution for holding down lofty materials, such as faux fur.

- Ideal as a topping for water-sensitive materials like wool and silk.

- Ideal as a backing for sheer materials with no stabilizer show-through.

- For each brand and type, follow the manufacturer's directions, as they may vary slightly from one to the next.

As a topper, heat-away makes it easier to stitch on lofty materials. Design from Teen Rock by OESD.

SPECIALTY

About

The stabilizers that fit into this category offer unique functionalities not provided by the other types. Each of these varieties are either cut away or left in the project and are used to add body or cover stitches.

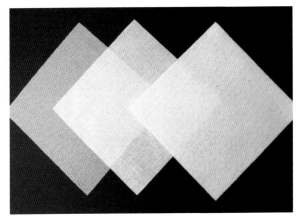

Specialty stabilizers offer specific functionalities that other types do not.

Varieties

Fusible tricot cut-away: Lightweight knit, sheer, and fusible. Ideal as a permanent backing prior to machine embroidering on delicate materials such as silks and satins to add body without changing the hand. Also works well as a backing to cover stitches and protect sensitive skin, such as on baby garments.

- OESD™—Gentle Touch Backing

- Exquisite® by dime—Fuse So Soft
- Sulky®—Tender Touch™

Fusible woven cut-away: Lightweight woven fusible. Ideal as a permanent backing prior to machine embroidering on light- to medium-weight materials such as quilting cotton. Helps prevent puckering. Can use in addition to other stabilizers, including tear-away and cut-away.

- OESD™—Fusible Woven
- Exquisite® by dime—Stretchy Knit Stabilizer

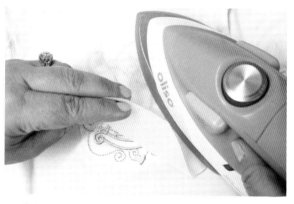

Here, fusible tricot cut-away covers the backside of the stitches on a baby onesie.

Embroidery fleece/batting: Lightweight batting. Note that the OESD™ version has a fusible backing that is ideal for certain embroidery projects in which you want to fuse ahead of time. Works well for In-the-Hoop bags, coin purses, stuffed animals, mug rugs, and the like—projects in which you would hoop the embroidery fleece as the stabilizer rather than hooping another stabilizer and floating the embroidery fleece on top. When it comes to In-the-Hoop projects, follow the designer's instructions and stabilizer suggestions.

- OESD™—Fuse and Fleece
- The Gypsy Quilter® Stitcher Series Hoop Easy Embroidery Batting
- HoopSisters—Battilizer®

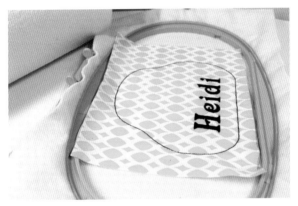

Embroidery fleece, or batting, works well as a hooped stabilizer for In-the-Hoop projects. Hexi Coin Purse by Sue O'Very Designs.

TIPS

Some specialty stabilizers are slightly heavier than others, so make adjustments according to the project. Follow the manufacturer's directions for each brand and type, as they may vary slightly from one to the next.

STABILIZER CHEAT SHEET		TEAR-AWAY
Woven	**Little to no stretch**	
	Quilt cotton	B=M, 1-2 or F or S
	Denim	B=M or S
	Canvas	B=M, H, or S
	Linen	B=L-M, F or S
	Gauze	B=L or F or S
Knit	**20% or higher stretch**	
	Onesie/light T-shirt	
	Pique polo/heavy T-shirt/ sweatshirt	
	Swimwear	
	Performance	
Napped	**Loft or pile**	
	Terrycloth (i.e., bath towel)	B=M or S
	Faux fur/velvet	B=S and M-H
	Fleece/minky	B=M, H, or S
Sheer	**See-thru or opaque**	
	Organza/chiffon	
	Lace/netting	
Non-woven	**No woven structure**	
	Cork	B=M or S
	Vinyl	B=L-M or S
	Pet screen	
Specialty	**Project-based**	
	Freestanding lace	
	Hard-to-hoop items	B=S
	In-the-Hoop projects	**

**Depends on project; follow suggested stabilizer types from designer

CUT-AWAY	WASH-AWAY	HEAT-AWAY	SPECIALTY
			*B=F/W or *B=F/R
B=M-H, S	T=L, Clear		*B=F/R
			*B=F/R
	T=L, Clear		*B=F/R
	B=S or B=Mesh, T=L, Clear		
B=F, Mesh, 1-2	T=L, Clear		*T/C, after emb
B=M-H, 1-2, or S	T=L, Clear	*T=Clear	
B=Mesh or M, 1-2	*T=L, Clear		*T/C, after emb
B=Mesh, 1-2			
	T=L, Clear	*T=Clear	
B=S	B=S, T=L, Clear	*T=Clear	
B=M or Mesh	T=L, Clear	*T=Clear	
	B=Mesh or B=S or B=H, Clear		
	B=L, Clear or B=Mesh and T=L, Clear		
	*T=L, Clear		
	B=S or B=H, Clear		
	B=Mesh or B=H, Clear 1-2		
B=S	B=S *T=L, Clear	*T=Clear	
**	**	**	**

L = Lightweight, M = Medium weight, H = Heavy weight, F = Fusible, S = Sticky, B = Backing, T = Topping,
F/W = Fusible woven, T/C = Fusible tricot, F/R = Flame retardant, Numbers = How many layers, * = Optional

Resources

In addition to the author's website (Sue O'Very Designs: *www.SueOVeryDesigns.com*), check out the following sources for inspiration, information, and helpful products.

All About Blanks: *www.allaboutblanks.com*

BERNINA: *www.bernina.com*

Bosal: *www.bosalonline.com*

Clover: *www.clover-usa.com*

Dritz: *www.dritz.com*

Exquisite by dime: *www.shop.dzgns.com*

Famore Cutlery: *www.famorecutlery.com*

GooGone: *www.googone.com*

The Gypsy Quilter Stitcher Series, Hoop Easy: *www.gypsyquilter.com*

HoopSisters: *www.hoopsisters.com*

Odif: *www.odifusa.com*

OESD: *www.embroideryonline.com*

Oliso: *www.oliso.com*

SCHMETZ: *www.schmetzneedles.com*

Scissortail Stitches: *www.scissortailstitches.com*

Sewline: *www.sewline.com.au*

SewTites: *www.sewtites.com*

Shannon Fabrics: *www.shannonfabrics.com*

Sulky: *www.sulky.com*

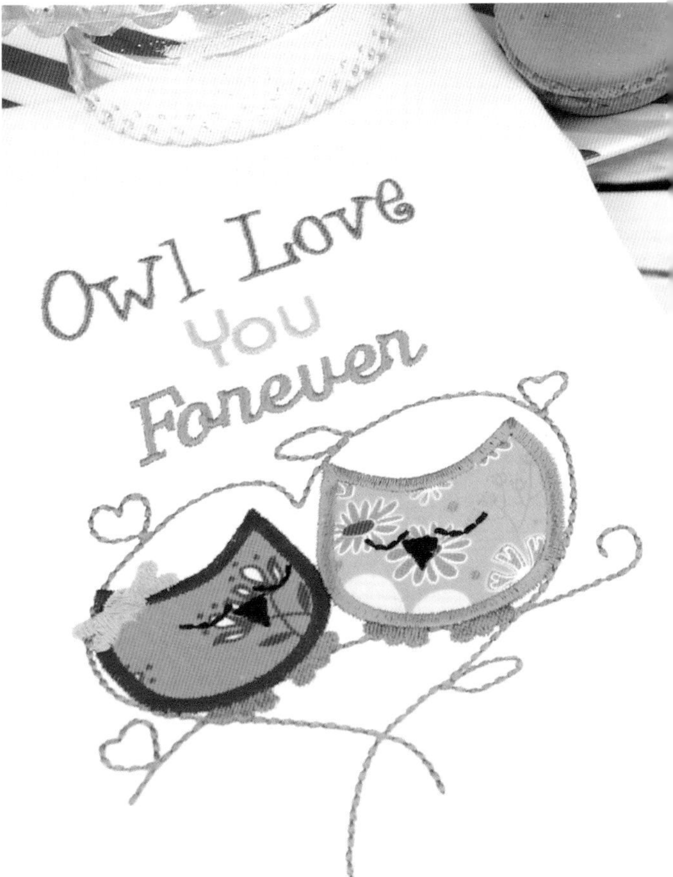
Owl Love
You
Forever

About the Author

Sue O'Very-Pruitt is known for her fresh style and love
for all things sewing. Whether on her YouTube channel
(*SueOVeryTV.com*), in her blog posts, or when teaching in-person,
Sue has a knack for simplifying sewing and making the many
details memorable and easy to understand. Drawing on her degree
in fashion design, her experience in leather work, and years of
designing and making costumes, she enjoys teaching beginners
how to sew and all the essential skills they need to know—from
fundamental sewing techniques to working with stabilizers and
notions to machine embroidery. With the love and support of
her husband, Joey, and her daughter, Heidi, Sue continues to
create new and clever ways to bring machine embroidery to her
audience. You can find Sue on Instagram, Pinterest, and Facebook
@SueOVeryDesigns and on her website *www.SueOVeryDesigns.com*.